MW01615968

THE WORLD'S BEST SPORTS JOKES

by Russ Edwards
and Jack Kreismer

RED-LETTER PRESS, INC.

SADDLE RIVER, NEW JERSEY

Red-Letter Press, Inc.

P.O. Box 393, Saddle River, N.J. 07458

www.Red-LetterPress.com

ACKNOWLEDGMENTS

Project Development Coordinator:
Kobus Reyneke

Cover design and typography:
s.w.artz, inc.

INTRODUCTION

It's in the nature of sports that somebody has to lose
but with **THE WORLD'S BEST SPORTS JOKES**,
every fan is a winner.

This volume of "Mr. Jokes" is jam-packed with more
corkers than Albert Belle's former bat collection. Filled
with gags that are in a league of their own, everyone is
guaranteed to have a ball.

Whether your favorite team just lost the Super Bowl
or you just took a bath in the office pool, this book will
have you batting a thousand at the tailgate party,
sports bar or water cooler.

THE WORLD'S BEST SPORTS JOKES

MR. JOKES

Wisecracks for Wiseguys

Two pigskin players are taking a college entrance exam:

Player 1– Psst, Bubba. Gimme the answer to
    number 22 where it says "Fill in the blank–
    Old MacDonald had a what?

Player 2– Farm, you idiot.

Player 1– How do you spell it?

Player 2– E-I-E-I-O.

The way a man plays tennis can be very
revealing. I was playing tennis with a man
I had been dating for a while and noticed
his reluctance to keep score properly. He
couldn't say, "Thirty-love." He kept saying,
"Thirty, I really like you but still have to see
other people."

                                                –RITA RUDNER

On the day of the race, a lot of people want you to sign something just before you get in the car so that they can say they got your last autograph.

-A.J. FOYT

The high school history class was assigned to name who they each considered to be the eleven greatest Americans. As the students were compiling their list, at one point the teacher noticed that Herbie looked perplexed. "Having a tough time?" the teach asked.

"I've got all but one," answered Herbie. "I just can't decide on the quarterback."

Q: *What do you get when you cross Shaquille O'Neal and a groundhog?*

A: *Six more weeks of basketball.*

"obSIRvations"

Old age is when you resent the swimsuit issue of "Sports Illustrated" because there are fewer articles to read.

-George Burns

I occasionally get birthday cards from fans. But it's often the same message: They hope it's my last.

-FORMER NATIONAL LEAGUE UMPIRE AL FORMAN

Men own basketball teams. Every year cheerleaders' outfits get tighter and briefer, and professional players' shorts get baggier and baggier.

-RITA RUDNER

"obSIRvations"

One loss is good for the soul. Too many losses are not good for the coach.

-Knute Rockne

And then there was the "not-too-bright" athlete who won a gold medal at the Olympics ... He was so proud he had it bronzed.

Arny and Barney were talking about their favorite sport. "How come you don't go fishing with Waldo anymore?" Arny asked Barney.

"Well, would you go fishing with someone who was loud, obnoxious, drank all the beer and kept capsizing the boat?"

"No," replied Arny. "I certainly would not."

"Well," said Barney, "neither will Waldo."

Take boxing, the simplest, stupidest sport of all. It's almost as if these two guys are just desperate to compete with each other, but they couldn't think of a sport. So they said, "Why don't we just pound each other for forty-five minutes? Maybe someone will come watch that."

-JERRY SEINFELD

I started boxing for exercise, and on the
very first day, the trainer got in the ring
with me and said, "Whoever controls the
breathing in the ring controls the fight."
I immediately passed out.

-GARRY SHANDLING

Ernie: What position does your brother play on
        the the football team?

Bernie: I'm not positive, but I think he's one of
        the drawbacks.

Q: What do you call a football player who
   becomes a born-again Christian?

A: A two-point conversion.

A guy bets big money on the horses. Every dollar he makes is spent at the track. One day his wife becomes very ill and is rushed to the hospital. The inveterate gambler goes to a friend and says, "Please, you've gotta help me. I'm gonna need some money to pay for my wife's hospital bills."

"I'm not loaning you anything, pal. You'll just blow it all on the horses."

"No, I won't! I swear!" says the gambler. "I've got money for the horses."

I play on New York City's only women's hockey team. We do play rough. We have checking. The only difference between men's and women's hockey is that women check, but then they apologize.

-LYNN HARRIS

My tennis coach told me I was one year away from being a good player. And next year, I'll be two years away.

-KEN POLISH

"obSIRvations"

The world's coming to an end.
The world's best golfer is black,
and the world's best rapper is white.

-Chris Rock

A golfing fanatic married a woman whose favorite pastime was attending auctions. Both husband and wife habitually talked in their sleep. One night the golfer yelled, "Fore."

His wife immediately countered, "Four fifty!"

Two visitors from Greece went to a baseball game. After a few innings, one turned to the other and asked, "Do you have any idea what this is all about?" The other replied, "No, it's all English to me."

Maybe you've heard about the boxing referee who used to work for NASA ... Every time a fighter got knocked down, he'd start counting "10, 9, 8..."

I competed in the long jump, because it seemed to be the only event where afterward you didn't fall down and throw up.

-DAVE BARRY

Terrell Owens, Tom Brady and Jerry Rice are standing before God at the Pearly Gates. The Lord looks at them and says, "Before I grant you a place at my side, I must first ask you what you believe in."

He asks Brady, "What is it that you believe?"

The Patriots quarterback looks at God and says with great passion, "I've been a Super Bowl winner more than once and I believe I have brought great joy to the fans of New England as a result. I believe in good sportsmanship on the field at all times and I think I've done that. More importantly, I believe one needs a strong sense of morals and values off the field and I would hope you think I've exhibited that, God."

"That I do, Mr. Brady. Take the seat to my left...And you, Mr. Rice?"

"Well, Lord, you know all things. You're well aware of the many records I set, primarily due to the fact I've always kept in the greatest shape possible. Indeed, I believe in keeping the body and mind as sound as possible."

"*That you've done, Mr. Rice. I'm proud of you. You may take the seat to my right...And you, Mr. Owens. What do you believe?*"

"*I believe you're in my seat.*"

You know horses are smarter than people. You never heard of a horse going broke betting on people.

-*Will Rogers*

My mom is eighty years old and still bowling. Yesterday she got three strikes. One was even in her lane.

-SCOTT WOOD

I went through life as a player to be named later.

-JOE GARAGIOLA

All pro athletes are bilingual.
They speak English and profanity.

-Gordie Howe

The psychology professor was giving a lesson on manic depression.

He asked the class, "What would you call someone who paces back and forth nervously, screams at the top of his lungs one minute, then sits in a chair sobbing uncontrollably the next?"

A jock from the rear of the class yells out, "I know...a basketball coach."

Did you hear about the short music afficionado who tried out for the Olympics?

He's a compact disc thrower.

The diehard sports fan told his friend, "I've gotta cut down on hot dogs and beer."

"How come?"

"Because I'm starting to get a ballpark figure."

Unlike in other sports, in tennis if you are getting killed you are expected to stay out there and continue to get killed.

-BILL COSBY

Go jogging? And get hit by a meteor?

-ROBERT BENCHLEY

Little Johnny was in his kindergarten class when the teacher asked the kids what their dads did for a living.

The usual jobs came up- fireman, salesman, accountant, policeman- but Johnny was uncharacteristically shy about giving an answer.

Finally, the teacher said, "Johnny, how about you? What does your father do for a living?"

Johnny murmured, "My dad's an exotic dancer."

The startled teacher quickly ended that segment of class and sent the other kids off to do some coloring. Then she took little Johnny aside and said, "Is that really true about your father?"

"No," said Johnny, "he plays for the Montreal Expos but I was too embarrassed to say it."

Q: How many college basketball players does it take to screw in a light bulb?

A: One...but he gets three credits for it.

And then there was the fighter they called Kid Cousteau, so named because he took so many dives.

In the Bowling Alley of Tomorrow, there will even be machines that wear rental shoes and throw the ball for you. Your sole function will be to drink beer.

-DAVE BARRY

At the summer Olympic Games, a girl bumped into a guy carrying an eight-foot long stick.

"Excuse me," said the girl, "but are you by any chance a pole vaulter?"

"Nein, I'm a German, but how did you know my name is Valter?"

Maybe you've heard about the jockey who was a tremendous overeater. He kept putting a la carte before the horse.

You can make a lot of money playing golf. Just ask my ex-wives.

-LEE TREVINO

A guy comes home from work, plops himself onto the Barcalounger in the family room, grabs the remote, and flips on the football game on the big screen TV. He yells into the kitchen, "Honey, bring me a cold one before it starts."

His wife brings him a can of beer. A few minutes later, he calls out to the wife again, "Honey, bring me another beer before it starts."

Again, his wife brings him a beer.

A short time later, he yells a third time, "Honey, bring me another beer before it starts."

The wife, now exasperated, marches into the family room and says, "You bum. I've been doing the wash... the dishes... the ironing...and now I'm waiting on you hand and foot!"

The husband says, "Oh, my God! It's started already!"

A man bought four box seats to a World Series game for he and his three sons. When they arrived at the ballpark, the man told his kids he had to use the men's room. Meanwhile, the boys meandered down to their seats only to find a man sprawled out on them.

"Excuse me, sir," said one of the boys timidly, "but I think these are our seats."

"Aaaaaaaaaaaggggghhhhh," stammered the man.

All three of the boys got scared and ran up the steps. They met their father, who was on his way back from the men's room, and told him what had happened. The father went down to the seats to confront the man himself.

"Excuse me, buddy, but I paid top dollar for these seats. You'll have to leave."

The man remained prostrate on the seats and again responded, "Aaaaaaaaaaggggghhhhh!"

At this point, the father decided to complain to an

usher who apologized for the inconvenience and promised to take care of the problem. The usher went down to the seats, approached the man and said, "Excuse me, sir. What's your name?"

"Geee–oooo–rrrr–ggg–e."

"Oh, George, where do you come from? asked the usher.

"Uuuuuupppppppstairs."

My dad is not real bright. But I love the guy. We go into this trophy shop because my basketball team won second place. We were in this shop and there are trophies everywhere. My dad looks around and goes, "This guy is really good."

-FRED WOLF

A baseball park is the one place where a man's wife doesn't mind his getting excited over somebody else's curves.

-BRENDAN FRANCIS

This is the first time Mike got up to Chapter 11 in anything.

-Jay Leno,
on Mike Tyson's
filing for bankruptcy

Q: *What happens if you hit a green golf ball into the Red Sea?*

A: *It gets wet.*

A couple of guys were sitting behind two nuns at a Red Sox game at Fenway. The nuns were dressed in habits and the guys were having a tough time seeing over their tops. At one point, they decided to antagonize the nuns to get them to move. One guy loudly says to the other, "I think I'd like to move to Texas. I hear there are very few Catholics there."

The other guy, speaking loudly enough for the nuns to hear, says, "I hear there are even fewer Catholics in Georgia. I certainly wouldn't mind going there."

One of the nuns turns around and matter-of-factly says, "Why don't you go to Hell? There aren't any Catholics there."

All I'm asking for is what I want.

-RICKEY HENDERSON

A Braves fan, Cubs fan, Yankees fan and Red Sox fan went rock climbing one day. All the way up the mountain, they were arguing about who was the most die-hard fan.

When they reached the top, the Atlanta fan jumped off the mountain in sacrifice as he yelled proudly, "This is for the Braves...Geronimo-o-o-o!"

Not to be outdone, the Chicago fan committed a "Harry Caray" as he too made the ultimate leap of faithfulness from the mountaintop.

Without a flinch, the staunch Yankee backer shouted, "The curse of the Bambino continues!" and pushed the Red Sox fan off the mountain.

If God didn't want man to hunt,
he wouldn't have given us plaid shirts.

-JOHNNY CARSON

If a woman has to choose between catching a fly ball and saving an infant's life, she will choose to save the infant's life without even considering if there are men on base.

-DAVE BARRY

"obSIRvations"

Baseball players are smarter than football players. How many times do you see a baseball team penalized for too many men on the field?

-Jim Bouton

What do you get if you cross a sportscaster with a common vegetable?

A common tater.

Rabid fan: A guy who boos a television set.

-JIMMY CANNON

A sports nut was strolling along the Cleveland shores of Lake Erie when he spotted a bottle floating in the water. As it drifted ashore, he picked it up and out popped a Genie.

"Master, Master," said the Genie, I am eternally grateful that you have released me from my bondage in this bottle. It has been ages since I've experienced freedom. For your reward, ask any three wishes and I will grant them to you."

The guy thought for a moment and said, "I would like for three things to happen this year- for the Indians to win the World Series, the Cavs to win the NBA title, and the Browns to win the Super Bowl."

The genie pondered this for a second- and then jumped back in the bottle.

A 44-year old man, who was born on May 4th, has been married for 4 years, has 4 kids, earns $44,444.44 a year, and who's lucky number is 4, gets a racing tip from a buddy. He's told that a horse named 4 Leaf Clover will be running in the fourth race in the number 4 spot at the local track that evening. The man hurries to the bank, withdraws $4,444.44, goes to the races and bets it all on 4 Leaf Clover in the 4th.

Sure enough, the horse comes in 4th.

I went to see a NASCAR race. Where did they get that name? Did two guys in North Carolina try to impress each other? "Hey Bubba, look at mah new Chevrolet." "WHOOOEEEE nahhhhssssscar."

-DOBIE MAXWELL

They say you can't do it, but remember, that
doesn't always work.

-CASEY STENGEL

The trouble with officials is they just
don't care who wins.

-Tommy Canterbury

A drunk staggered into a local gym where he
saw a fighter shadow-boxing in the middle of the
boxing ring. A few seconds after watching the boxer
dance and punch the air, the drunk called out to
the fighter, "Hey! You might as well quit fightin'.
The other guy's gone!"

One day during recess, the new elementary school counsellor, Mrs. Jones, noticed that little Johnny was all by himself on one side of the playground while all the other kids were playing soccer at the other end. Mrs. Jones asked Johnny if something was bothering him. Johnny said, "There aint nuthin' bothering me, ma'am."

A bit later, Mrs. Jones noticed that Johnny was in the same spot, again, all by his lonesome. She went up to him and said, "Would you like me to be your friend?"

Johnny eyed her suspiciously, then said, "Well, I guess so."

Now Mrs. Jones felt she was making some headway so she asked, "Why are you standing here all by yourself?"

"Because," Johnny said with a good deal of frustration, "I'm the damn goalie!"

When primitive man beat the ground with sticks, they called it witchcraft. When modern man does the same thing, they call it golf.

-MICHAEL NEARY

Q: Why did the Packers and Bears have to re-surface their fields?

A: Too much Moss in the end zone.

Baseball Player #1: How'd you make out with the owner's daughter?

Baseball Player #2: Horrible…no hits, no runs, no heiress.

The punch drunk fighter was nearly killed in a horse riding mishap. He fell from the horse and was almost trampled to death. Fortunately, the Kmart manager came out and unplugged it.

"obSIRvations"

The first word you see in every airport is terminal.

*-ESPN analyst Beano Cook,
about his fear of flying*

You can pitch a gem and lose, but you can't lose when you win...wait, don't quote me on that. I sound like Yogi Berra.

-FORMER PITCHER ERIC SHOW

A clerk working part-time in a grocery store was having a difficult time with a customer who kept insisting on buying only half a head of lettuce. Finally, the employee went to his manager and said, "Boss, there's some idiot in the produce department who wants only a half a head of lettuce."

Then, out of the corner of his eye he saw the customer standing directly behind him so he quick-wittedly said, "And this gentleman would like to buy the other half."

After the customer was satisfactorily taken care of, the manager praised the clerk for his quick-thinking and asked, "Where are you from?"

He replied, "From Montreal, the city of hockey players and loose women."

The manager shouted, "Hey, my wife's from Montreal!"

"Which team?" said the clerk.

The Super Bowl committee has been exploring international possibilities for the event. Among the host sites considered was the new stadium in Warsaw but that was quickly dismissed with the realization that no matter where you sat you'd be behind a Pole.

Then there was the horse that came in so late the jockey was wearing pajamas.

It's not whether you win or lose, but who gets the blame.

-FORMER DALLAS COWBOYS
LINEMAN BLAINE NYE

Doc, I need help," says Mort to the psychiatrist. "It may sound strange but I keep thinking that I'm a horse."

"I think I can cure you," the psychiatrist answers, "but it's going to take some time and it's going to be extremely expensive."

"Money's not a problem, Doc. I just won the Kentucky Derby."

Then there was the Russian tennis player who's game was great at the nyet.

No one ever says: "It's only a game," when their team is winning.

-ED O'BRIEN

I say, why pay outrageous prices for ski trips when I can just stick my face in the freezer and fall down on the kitchen floor.

-JOHN WAGNER

Three guys desperately want to get into the Olympic stadium but the Games are sold out so they decide to pose as athletes. The first guy picks up a long piece of pipe, walks up to the athletes' entrance and says to the guard, "I'm a pole vaulter."

The guard lets him in.

The second guy appears with a manhole cover and says, "Discus thrower."

He's also allowed in.

The third guy shows up with some barbed wire and says, "Fencing."

Show me a good loser and I'll show you a man who is playing golf with his boss.

-JIM MURRAY

What Women Want: To be loved, to be listened to, to be desired, to be respected, to be needed, to be trusted, and sometimes, just to be held.

What Men Want: Tickets for the World Series.

-Dave Barry

Q: How do you know if you're really cross-eyed?

A: You can watch a tennis match without moving your head.

A guy goes to a psychiatrist and says, "Doc, I need help. I just can't seem to make decisions."

The doctor says, "Actually, that's not so unusual. Lots of people have a tough time making up their minds."

"Yeah, but I'm an umpire."

Every decade or so, I attempted to play tennis, and it always consists of thirty-seven seconds of actually hitting the ball and two hours of yelling. "Where did the ball go? "Over that condominium." With bowling, once you let go of the ball, it's no longer your legal responsibility. They have these wonderful machines that find it for you and send it right back.

-DAVE BARRY

Old placekickers never die, they just go on missing the point.

-HALL OF FAME KICKER
LOU "THE TOE" GROZA

A man goes to the racetrack and sees a priest making the sign of the cross on a horse. The horse goes on to win the first race. Before the second race, the priest blesses another horse, and it too comes in first.

The man figures he'll follow suit. He bets on each horse the priest blesses. When the last race comes up, the priest makes the sign of the cross over a horse. The man bets his whole fortune on the horse. The race starts. The horse drops dead as it leaves the gate. The man rushes to the priest and demands to know what went wrong. The priest says, "Son, don't you know the difference between a blessing and the last rites?"

An avid football fan was hollerin' and hootin' all game long. He grew more and more hoarse as the pigskin contest went on until finally, in the fourth quarter, he whispered to the guy sitting next to him, "I think I've lost my voice."

The other guy replied, "Don't worry. You'll find it in my right ear."

Golf is one of the few sports where a white man can dress like a black pimp.

-Robin Williams

I pulled a hamstring during the New York City Marathon. An hour into the race I jumped up off the couch.

-DAVID LETTERMAN

Beethoven's Ninth Symphony was being performed at the famed Carnegie Hall. During intermission, the conductor becomes frantic when he realizes the last few pages of his sheet music are missing. After telling his assistant this, the trusted aide remembers that the missing pages were accidentally locked in the dressing room. He assures the conductor that they'll be on his music stand in time for when they are needed.

"I would hope so," growls the conductor. "And while you're at it, keep an eye on the bass players. They've been drinking ever since the intermission started."

The conductor then goes about his business while the assistant makes sure the bass players down a few cups of coffee before they return to their orchestra seats.

As the curtain rises for the remainder of the symphony, the assistant rushes to find a security guard who can open the dressing room. He finds one and hurries him down to the locked room.

"What's all the fuss about?" asks the security guard.

The assistant replies, "It's the bottom of the ninth, the score is tied, and the bassists are loaded!"

A Jewish football player received a scholarship to Notre Dame. When there was a semester break, he flew home. His rabbi bumped into him at the airport. Aware that the player was a member of the Fighting Irish football team the rabbi said, "Tell me, son. They haven't converted you to their ways, have they?"

The football star answered, "Why, no...absolutely not, Father!"

I like sports because I enjoy knowing that many of these macho athletes have to vomit before a big game. Any guy who would take a job where you gotta puke first is my kinda guy.

-GEORGE CARLIN

Some parents got into a brawl at their kids'
soccer match in New Jersey. They said
they were just teaching their children
European soccer.

-CRAIG KILBORN

Q: What's the difference between a Yankee
Stadium hotdog and a Wrigley Field hotdog?

A: You can buy a Yankee Stadium hotdog in
October.

Did you hear about the pitcher and his expectant wife?
They both suffered from complete exhaustion in the ninth.

A horse shows up at an open tryout for the New York Yankees. The manager doesn't take the horse too seriously, but nonetheless, allows him to take some swings in the batting cage. Much to his surprise, the horse is an unbelievable power hitter and after clubbing ten homers in a row the Yankees decide to sign him up.

That night, the horse is sitting on the bench. In the bottom of the ninth, with two men out and the Yankees trailing 2-1, the horse is called on to pinch-hit. He steps up to the plate, cracks the first pitch off the centerfield wall and just stands there.

Everyone in the dugout is standing and yelling, "Run! Run!"

The horse say, "Run! Hrrmmmmph! If I could run, I'd be at Aqueduct."

I never cease to amaze myself. I say this humbly.

-DON KING

Colts coach Tony Dungy is upset over his team's recent losing streak so he decides to visit Bill Belichick at a New England practice. "Coach, how is it that the Patriots always seem to be on a roll? What's your secret?"

Belichick says, "Watch this." He calls over Tom Brady and says, "Tom, who's your father's brother's nephew?"

Brady responds, "That's easy, coach…me."

Belichick turns to Dungy and says, That's what it takes, Tony- a smart quarterback. You've got to have a smart QB."

Dungy returns to Indianapolis and at the next Colts' workout calls over Peyton Manning. "Manning," Dungy barks, "Who's your father's brother's nephew?"

Manning looks baffled, then asks, "Uh, can I get back to you on that, Coach?"

Annoyed, Dungy says, "Make it quick."

During practice, Manning asks Edgerrin James, "Edgerrin, Coach just asked me a strange question: Who's your father's brother's nephew?"

James answers, "Duuuh, that' simple. It's me."

Later on, Manning catches up with Dungy and says, "Coach, I think I've got it. My father's brother's nephew is Edgerrin James."

Dungy, exasperated, says, "No, no, no ... It's Tom Brady!"

I've been watching the Classic Sports Network lately, and I must say, the Chicago Bears are looking good in 1985. Also, keep an eye out for a young coach named Vince Lombardi in the fifties - he's got something!

-BOB ODONKIRK

A lot of horses get distracted. It's just human nature.

-NICK ZITO, TRAINER OF 1994 KENTUCKY DERBY
WINNER GO FOR GIN

Then there was the football matchup between two last place teams. It was called the Game of the Weak.

A Boston marathoner suffered a sudden spell of dizziness so he stopped for a minute and rested his head between his legs.

Seeing this, a preppy Harvard student asked in very proper fashion, "Have you vertigo?"

The marathoner said, "Yes. Four more miles."

Q: *What's the difference between a football and Prince Charles?*

A: *One's thrown to the air, the other heir to the throne.*

Old place-kickers never die, they just go on missing the point.

-Hall of Fame kicker
Lou "The Toe" Groza

Women are now referees for the NBA, and they're driving some guys crazy. They don't just call a foul, they want to talk about why it happened.

-LESLIE NESBITT

Owner Al Davis had put together an almost-perfect Raiders football team. The only thing missing was a top-flight quarterback. Davis had his scouts visit all the colleges and high schools, but the pickings were slim.

Alas, one evening while watching the network news, he saw a war-zone scene in Iraq. In the background of the video, Davis spotted an Iraqui soldier with a magnificent arm. He hurled a hand grenade right into a 12fth-floor window 150 yards away. Then he threw another into a group of soldiers 200 yards away – kaboom!!! Time after time, the soldier demonstrated perfect accuracy tossing the "bomb."

Davis said to himself, "I've got to get this guy. He could finally bring us to a Super Bowl."

The Raiders' owner made arrangements to bring the Iraqui soldier to America. The Oakland brain trust taught the young man the game of football and, lo and behold, the Raiders won the Super Bowl!

After the big event, when Davis asked the Super

Bowl MVP what he wanted, other than a trip to Disney World, the young quarterback replied, "I'd just like to talk to my mother."

So the former Iraqui soldier's mom was called and, on national TV, she said, "I don't want to talk to you. You deserted us. As far as I'm concerned, you are not my son."

Well, now the young man was beside himself. "Maybe you don't understand, Mom," he said. "I just won the biggest sports event in the whole world."

"No, I don't think you understand," retorted his mom. "As we speak, there's gunfire all around us. The neighborhood is in shambles. Your brother was beaten beyond recognition last week. I won't even tell you what almost happened to me."

The young man's mom then paused to regain her composure and said, "I'll never forgive you for making us move to Oakland."

I think sports stars make great role models,
particularly if you are thinking about a
career in crime.

-LAURA KIGHTLINGER

Have you heard about the collegiate football star who's been an undergraduate for eight years?

He can run and tackle with the best of them...but he can't pass.

Q: What do you call a New Orleans Saint wearing a Super Bowl ring?

A: Thief

Ralph was playing table tennis with a guy who had a super duper slam shot. In a freak accident, one such shot rammed right down Ralph's mouth. He was rushed to the hospital, given a local anesthetic and then the doctor began to perform surgery.

First he cut into Ralph's left side, then his right, then up into his chest and down into his belly.

Ralph shrieked, "Doc, why all the incisions!?!"

"That's just the way the ball bounces."

There's a fine line between fishing
and just standing on the shore looking
like an idiot.

-STEVEN WRIGHT

I went to a Chinese bowling alley once.
I rented these great shoes, but you weren't
allowed to wear them inside.

-WENDY LIEBMAN

A guy goes to confession. He says, "Father, forgive me, for I have sinned. I was skiing when I saw my boss on the same slope. He didn't recognize me because I was wearing my ski mask so I skied over to where he was, pushed him and roared with laughter as he rolled over and over down the hill."

"Why are you telling me this again?" asks the priest. "That's the fifth time you've confessed this transgression."

The guy answers, "I know. I just like talking about it."

Q & A's

Q: How many sportscasters does it take to change a light bulb?

A: Two...one to change it and one to do color

Q: What happened to the two silkworms who had a match race?

A: They wound up in a tie.

Q: What's the difference between an umpire and a pickpocket?

A: An umpire watches steals...

Q: If a basketball team was running after a baseball team, what time would it be?

A: Five after nine

Q: What do you get when you cross a comedic actress with a hockey player?

A: Goalie Hawn

I was in Little League. I was on first base -
I stole third. I ran straight across the
diamond. Earlier in the week, I learned the
shortest distance between two points is a
straight line. I argued with the ump that
second base was out of my way.

-STEVEN WRIGHT

Q: *Why did they stop selling beer at the*
   doubleheader?

A: *Because the home team lost the opener*

How about the fighter nicknamed "Submarine
Sal"?
Seems he was always taking a dive.

Q: *What's the only creature that can take thousands of people for a ride at the same time?*

A: *A racehorse*

The secret of managing is to keep the guys who hate you away from the guys who are undecided.

-Casey Stengel

The fight was so short that when they raised the winner's arm, I thought it was a deodorant commercial.

-SLAPPY WHITE

I play tennis, and I'm pretty good, but no matter how much I practice I'll never be as good as a wall.

-MITCH HEDBERG

If one synchronized swimmer drowns, do all the rest have to drown too?

-Steven Wright

A fighter was in the ring with Siamese twins. After the bout he returned home and his wife asked, "Did you win?"

He answered, "Yes and no."

A guy from San Francisco, a guy from Detroit and a guy from Boston are granted a talk with God. They're each allowed one question. The guy from San Francisco inquires, "Will there ever be a time when we don't have to worry about earthquakes?"

God responds, "Yes, but not in your lifetime."

Then the guy from Detroit asks, "God, will there ever be a time when our city has no crime?"

Again God replies, "Yes, but not in your lifetime."

Finally, the guy from Boston asks, "God, will the Red Sox ever win the World Series?"

God answers, "Yes, but not in my lifetime!"

Old ski-jumpers never die, they simply lose their inclination.

-COLIN M. JARMAN

Q: What do you call the NFL's out-of-control Baltimore offensive lineman?

A: A Raven lunatic

Did you hear about the football brute who wrote "TGIF" on his cleats? He wanted to be reminded that "Toes Go In First."

A baseball game is twice as much fun if you're seeing it on the company's time.

-WILLIAM C. FEATHER

A guy with a little dog under his arm walks into a French Quarter bar in New Orleans one Sunday afternoon. He sits on a stool and places the dog on a stool beside him. A football game is on the television at the bar.

The guy orders a beer and asks the bartender, "What's the score of the Saints game? My dog and I are Saints fans."

The bartender says, "The Packers are leading thirteen to nuthin'."

No sooner did the bartender say that than the Saints returned a kickoff for a touchdown. The dog then stood up on the bar stool and started doing somersaults.

"Wow! That's really something," says the bartender.

"Oh, he does that every time the Saints score a touchdown," declares the dog's owner.

"If he does that for a touchdown, what does he do when the Saints win?"

The guy replies, "I wouldn't know. I've only had him for three years."

*My doctor, Nick the Knife, is a specialist ...
he specializes in cutting up my knees and
sticking needles into me. And he's really
painless - he doesn't feel any pain at all.*

-JOE NAMATH

You know the old rule: He who have
fastest cart never have to play bad lie.

-Mickey Mantle, on golf

Q: *Why is it so difficult to drive a golf ball?*
A: *Because it doesn't have a steering wheel*

The challenger was getting clobbered by the heavyweight champ. After the first round he stumbled back to his corner where his trainer said, "Let him hit you with left hooks in the second. Your face is crooked."

An angry homeowner says to a kid, "Have you seen who broke my window?"

The kid replies, "No but have you seen my baseball?"

Exactly how intricate a sport is jogging? You were two years old; you ran after the cat; you pretty much had it mastered.

-RICK REILLY

I don't get too excited about the Olympics.
In fact, I only watch about every four years.

-WENDY MORGAN

Muggsy and Buggsy had been together in Hell for many, many years. Their eternal job was to shovel coal into the fires side by side.

Suddenly, one day they felt cold air. The air got colder and colder. Snow began to fall. The next thing they knew, there was a blizzard. The snow blanketed the ground and extinguished the fires. Next, a gust of frigid wind froze over the entire surface of Hell!

"What the heck is going on here?" Muggsy wondered out loud.

Buggsy answered, "I don't know for sure, but I have a hunch that the Bills just won the Super Bowl."

Milt Famie was one of the top pitchers to have ever played for the Brewers. His only problem was his tolerance for alcohol. Famie could not hold the hard stuff so his teammates, coaches and friends always made sure he steered clear of it.

It was the night before a World Series game against the Yankees (who knew that Famie would be pitching against them the next afternoon). A few of the Yankees schemed a way to get Famie out of his hotel room and into the tavern next door by pretending to be movie producers who wanted to do a film on the hurler's life.

Famie had more than one too many beers at the tavern and, sure enough, the next day he couldn't find the plate. He walked the first six batters he faced before his manager mercifully removed him from the game. The two runs he gave up cost the Brewers the game as the Yankees won, 2-1.

During the postgame press conference, Joe Torre, the Yankees manager, was asked why he thought that the Brewers pitcher was so wild. Torre, aware of his players prank, slyly remarked, "It's the beer that made Milt Famie walk us."

A football fan is a guy who'll yell at the quarterback for not spotting an open receiver forty-five yards away, then head for the parking lot and not be able to find his own car.

-MIKE RYAN

Q: What's a football player with good intuition called?

A: A hunchback

Q: Why are boxers good at geometry?

A: Because they're used to circling in a squared ring

After Dallas Cowboys owner Jerry Jones dies and goes to heaven, God is taking him on a tour of the place. He shows Jerry a small three-bedroom home with a tiny Cowboys pennant hanging over the front porch.

"This is your eternal home, Jerry," says God. "You should feel mighty proud because most folks don't get their own private living quarters here."

Jerry looks at the home, then does an about face and sees this huge four-story mansion with two gigantic Oakland Raiders flags flying between the four marble pillars. And parked in the circular driveway is a black and silver limo with the Raiders logo on the hood.

"Thanks for my home, God," says Jerry, "but I have just one question. You give me this tiny home with a miniature Cowboys pennant and Al Davis gets that beautiful mansion. How come?

God laughs and says, "Oh, that's not Al Davis' home. That's mine."

I had this great idea to make the Great Wall of China into a handball court.

-GEORGE GOBEL

Then there was the pro football bruiser who was offered seven figures to pen his autobiography. A year later, he turned in the story of his Jeep.

Q: Why were the the Hawks the last NBA team to get a website?

A: Because they couldn't put up three W's in a row.

Football centers make snap decisions.

There exists an inverse correlation between the size of a ball and the quality of writing about the sport in which the ball is used. There are superb books about golf, very good books about baseball, not very many good books about football, very few good books about basketball, and there are no good books on beachballs.

-George Plimpton

I used to watch golf on television, but my doctor said that I needed more exercise. So now I watch tennis.

-DOUG DRAGON

I can't believe my rotten luck," moaned Mulligan. "I haven't had a winning horse in more than two months."

"Hey, maybe you should try out my system," said Hoolihan. "It's worked pretty well for me lately."

"What system is that?" asked Mulligan.

"Well," answered Hoolihan, "it's pretty simple. Every day that I plan on going to the track, that morning I go to church and pray for ten minutes. I've had at least two winners a day since I've been doing that."

Mulligan was ready to try anything so, sure enough, the next morning he went to church and prayed for half an hour. Then it was off to the racetrack. At the end of the day, he ran into Hoolihan.

"That system of yours is patooie!" he complained to Hoolihan. "I went to church this morning, prayed three times as long as you do and didn't have a single winner all afternoon."

"*Where did you go to church?*" asked Hoolihan.

"*To the one on Peach Street,*" said Mulligan.

"*You idiot!*" exclaimed Hoolihan. "*That church is for trotters.*"

The most important rule of horseshoes is, first remove the horse.

-*Milton Berle*

A friend gave me seats to the World Series. From where I sat, the game was just a rumor.

-HENNY YOUNGMAN

This just in. People who watch bowling:
People who watch golf laugh at you.

—CRAIG KILBORN

Riley says to his psychiatrist, "I'm obsessed with baseball, Doc. It's taken over my life. I eat, drink and think baseball. I even sleep baseball. I dream about it every night. The second I close my eyes I'm running the base paths, fielding a grounder or chasing a fly ball. I wake up more tired than before I went to bed. What can I do, Doc?"

The psychiatrist replies, "The first thing you have to do is to make a conscious effort not to think about the game. For example, when you close your eyes make believe you're watching the lottery results on TV and—wow!—you just won a million dollars!"

"What are you, nuts, Doc?" cries Riley. "I'll miss my turn at bat!"

Did you hear about the businessman who opened a combination bowling lane/basketball court?

He named it Alley Hoop.

Did you hear about the wide receiver named Cinderella?

Seems he kept missing the ball.

Skiing is the only sport where you can spend an arm and a leg to break an arm and a leg.

-HENRY BEARD

I don't think the discus will ever attract
any interest until we start throwing them
at each other.

-AL OERTER

The turtles and skunks decide to have a soccer match. The turtles' team is slow as molasses while the skunks' team just plain stinks. The game is scoreless with just seconds to go when, suddenly, a centipede—picked up as a ringer by the skunks—rushes onto the field, gets a pass, dribbles the ball, shoots and scores as the shell-shocked turtles watch the game go by the boards.

Afterwards, the coach of the skunks asks the centipede, "Where have you been all game?"

The centipede answers, "I was stringing up my cleats."

It's the state prison's championship game. There are two outs in the bottom of the ninth inning. The home team is down by one and the bases are loaded. The catcher walks out to the mound and says to the pitcher, "Take your time. You've got twenty years."

Q: Why was Cinderella a lousy football player?
A: Because she had a pumpkin for a coach

I play tennis, and I'm pretty good, but no matter how much I practice I'll never be as good as a wall.

-MITCH HEDBERG

SPORTS HOROSCOPE

Aquarius (Jan 20-Feb 18) The Office Pool
Born under the sign of the office pool, you can soon expect to pick up a bundle at the track. Just be sure to spread it around the rose bushes as soon as possible.

Pisces (Feb 19-Mar 20) The Protective Cup
The conjunction of Mars and Jupiter will bring you the "Most Valuable Player" award after the big game. Unfortunately, it'll be from your poker buddies.

Aries (Mar 21-Apr 19) The Beer Belly
All your friends consider you the biggest sports fan they know. That's because when it comes to blowing a lot of hot air around, you da' man!

Taurus (Apr 20-May 20) The Armchair Quarterback
The stars say you can expect to be on the cover of *Sports Illustrated.* Someone will leave it on the bench just before you sit down.

Gemini (May 21-Jun 21) The Ref
The transit of Neptune means that you're not all that athletic. Most guys stay in shape by pumping iron. Your idea of staying in shape is pumping gas.

Cancer (Jun 22-Jul 22) The Jock
Your softball skills will earn you much fame. You'll be invited to Times Square next New Year's Eve for a special honor...They'll want you to drop the ball.

Sports Horoscope

Leo (Jul 23-Aug 22) The Sports Bar
You spend so much time watching baseball, you actually believe that the last words to the national anthem are "Play Ball!"

Virgo (Aug 23-Sep 22) The Season Pass
Your talents will lead you to develop a new workout program for sports fans—"Beer-oebics"—zip, lift, chug, crunch, zip, lift, chug, crunch...

Libra (Sep 23-Oct 23) The Catcher's Mitt
You possess the physique of a champion skier... going downhill fast.

Scorpio (Oct 24-Nov 21) The Bench
When it comes to football, you'll play in the Ivy League. After every game, you'll wind up attached to an I-V.

Sagittarius (Nov 22-Dec 21) The Six Pack
Soon, your appearance on the field will hearten and inspire the entire team...too bad it's the opposing team.

Capricorn (Dec 22-Jan 19) The Groin Pull
The stars portend that you will some day be the starting pitcher for the New York Yankees. Of course, that will only be when the regular water boy is late.

Seventy-five percent of your body heat is lost through the top of your head. Which sounds like you could go skiing naked if you got a good hat.

-JERRY SEINFELD

Ruppert Nerdock, the newspaper magnate, spent oodles of money to buy a racehorse. The noted trainer Willie Shumaker offered to race his horse against Nerdock's. The night of the match race, the track was filled and sportswriters from all of Nerdock's newspapers were there. Unfortunately for Nerdock, his horse didn't live up to its billing and was beaten by nine lengths. The next day, the sports page headline on all of Nerdock's newspapers read:
NERDOCK'S HORSE FINISHES SECOND, SHUMAKER'S HORSE NEXT-TO-LAST.

A cricket ambled into a sporting goods store in London. The store's owner, somewhat taken aback to see a cricket with an interest in sports, said, "Hey, we have a popular game that goes by your name!"

"You're kidding," said the cricket. "You have a game called Jiminy?"

Q: What do you get if you cross a bowling lane with a famous heavyweight boxer?

A: Muhammad Alley

If you don't know where you're going, you could wind up someplace else.

-YOGI BERRA

I look on skiing as standing in an ice-cold shower while tearing up hundred-dollar bills.

-CHAD MORGAN

A lawyer was reading the will of a wealthy man to members of his family. As he neared the end of it, the lawyer read aloud, "And to my son Waldo, whom I promised to remember in my will even though he played golf all the time and never worked a day in his life...Hi there, Waldo!"

Maybe you've heard about the farmer who crossed his bookie with a hen...He got a chicken that laid odds.

Do you know about the fighter nicknamed "Rembrandt"?

His face was always on the canvas.

Nothing counts in golf like your opponent.

-Milton Berle

Anthropologists have discovered a 50-million-year-old human skull with three perfectly preserved teeth intact. They're not sure, but they think it may be the remains of the very first hockey player.

-JAY LENO

Last year I entered the Los Angeles Marathon. I finished last. It was embarrassing. And the guy who was in front of me, second to last, was making fun of me. He said, "How does it feel to come in last?" I said, "You want to know?" So I dropped out.

-GERRY BEDNOB

Then there was the 7'2" basketball star who got his height from his parents. They were each 3'7".

Maybe you've heard about the lousy fighter who was on the mat so often he wore out his welcome.

PUNCHLINES

Maybe you heard about the Mafioso type who
dubbed himself "The Pugilistic Engineer."
He made a career of fixing fights.

Then there was the colorful fighter.
He was black and blue all over.

A good fighter always considers the rights of others.

The toughest thing about fighting is
picking up your teeth with your boxing gloves on.

The fight manager nicknamed his boxer "Laundry"
...Seems he was always hanging over the ropes.

Fighters make money hand over fist.

Did you hear about the fighter who had the
misfortune of breaking his nose in two places?
He vowed never to go back to either of them.

Old skaters never die, they just lose their ice sight.

                                              -ERIC LEHMANN

Chess will be accepted as an Olympic sport in the 2008 Games. The other Olympic athletes are excited that the chess players are joining them, and say they're looking forward to giving them wedgies and taking their lunch money.

-CONAN O'BRIEN

A snail bought a particularly impressive race car and decided to enter the Indianapolis 500. To give the car a distinctive look, the snail had a big letter S painted on the hood, sides and trunk before the big race. When the race began, the snail's car immediately took the lead, prompting one of the spectators to say, "Look at that S car go!"

Former 49ers quarterback Steve Young was poked in the eye during a pileup. He went to the sideline where the trainer recommended he put on an eye patch. Young felt it might hurt his peripheral vision on one side so he refused. Before he went back into the game his coach advised him to rely on the peeper that was okay as he said,

"Remember, only the good eye, Young."

Monica Seles is using this really huge racket. What kind of sport is tennis where you can change the size of the equipment because you suck at it? How does that work? Why don't baseball players just put on really long shoes, so they're always safe?

-DAN WILSON

College football is a sport that bears the same relation to education that bullfighting does to agriculture.

-ELBERT HUBBARD

A bush league baseball player is trying to impress the superstar in spring training. He brags, "Hey, I use a limo wherever I go."

The superstar responds, "Is that so? How long have you been a chauffeur?"

And then there was the dim-witted race car driver who kept pulling into the pits to ask for directions.

A slick-fielding baseball player was walking by a burning building. A mother with a baby in her arms yelled to him from the third floor. The ballplayer told her to drop the baby. She let go, he caught the baby, then whirled and threw it to first base.

If you're a pro coach, NFL stands for "Not For Long."

-Jerry Glanville

College football would be more interesting if the faculty played instead of the students - there would be a great increase in broken arms, legs and necks.

-H.L. MENCKEN

I give the same half-time speech over and over. It works best when my players are better than the other coach's players.

-CHICK MILLS

If you see a defensive team with dirt and mud on their backs, they've had a bad day.

-John Madden

The English teacher instructed the class to write a composition about the national pastime. Wiseacre Wally turned in his paper just a few moments later. It read, "Game postponed due to rain."

Did you hear about the dentist who was an avid baseball fan? During the day he yanked at roots and at night he did just the opposite.

Q: How many Arizona Cardinals does it take the change a flat tire?

A: One, unless it's a blowout... Then the whole team shows up.

We can't win at home. We can't win on the road. As general manager, I just can't figure out where else to play.

-PAT WILLIAMS, THEN GENERAL MANAGER OF THE ORLANDO MAGIC

The most favorite activity of nudists:
volleyball. The least favorite: dodge ball.

-JAY LENO

A baseball player died and went to Heaven. Once up there, he was able to look down to Hell where he saw the most spectacular stadium with a capacity crowd, players on the field and a batter at the plate. "Boy, St. Peter," the ballplayer said. "It looks like a game is just about to start. You call that Hell? I'd love to be playing there."

"That's just it," smiled St. Peter. "So would they, but they don't have a ball."

A not too bright boxer pleaded with his manager. "Listen to me. I'm in great shape. I been trainin' for eight months. My eatin' and drinkin' habits are great. I been goin' ta bed early and gettin' a good night's sleep every night. I'm tellin' ya, I've trained and trained and trained. Please, please...ya gotta let me fight Lefty Looie."

His manager responded, "If I told you once, I told you a million times...you are Lefty Looie!"

One of my favorite Olympic events is the luge. This is on the bobsled run, but there's no sled. It's just Bob. It's just a human being hanging on for dear life.

-JERRY SEINFELD

There's always one of my uncles who watches a boxing match with me and says, "Sure. Ten million dollars. You know, for that kind of money, I'd fight him." As if someone is going to pay two hundred dollars a ticket to see a fifty-seven-year-old carpet salesman get hit in the face once and cry.

-LARRY MILLER

There was a very old fighter who had trouble sleeping. His doctor advised him, "Just lie down, relax and start counting to 100."

A week later the guy came back to the doctor and said, "It's no use. I keep getting up at the count of nine."

*And then there was the golfer who had an
excellent short game. Unfortunately, it was off
the tee.*

Swimming isn't a sport. It's just a way
to keep from drowning. Riding a bus
isn't a sport; so why should sailing be a
sport? Tennis is just ping-pong while
standing on the table.

-George Carlin

*Our team was surprisingly consistent
this year. We closed with a seven-seven
record. We lost seven at home, and seven
on the road.*

-STEVE WHEELER

I'm a football fan, but I think there are too
many games on over the holidays. At our
Thanksgiving dinner, Dolores passed me the
turkey and I spiked it.

-BOB HOPE

Q: *What do you get when you cross a football*
   player with someone who lives in a church
   bell tower?

A: *The Halfback of Notre Dame*

Did you hear about the giant basketball player
who became a prizefighter? He developed a
cauliflower navel.

The Pope arrived at the Pearly Gates where St. Peter took him to his apartment...a small, one-room unit. As the Pontiff was settling in, he looked out the window and saw a limousine pull up in front of a mansion across the heavenly street. A big, burly guy dressed to the nines got out of the limo and was escorted by a couple of female angels into the palatial home.

"Wow! Who is that?" asked the Pope.

"Oh, that's Big John McFarland," replied St. Peter. "He was a baseball umpire."

"A baseball umpire?" the Pope said. "My gosh, I was the head of the Roman Catholic Church and all I've got is this tiny room. What magnanimous thing must he have done to be granted with such rewards?"

"To tell you the truth," answered St. Peter, "we have a whole bunch of popes up here, but McFarland is the first umpire we've had in centuries."

*If you're not into sports, guys think you're
less of a man unless you can account for
time in activities equally masculine. When
they ask, "Wanna go see the game?" I reply,
"I can't. I gotta go put a transmission in a
stripper's car."*

-BOB NICKMAN

Ralph was playing table tennis with a guy who
had a super duper slam shot. In a freak accident,
one such shot rammed right down Ralph's mouth.
He was rushed to the hospital where a doctor
performed emergency surgery.

First he cut into Ralph's left side, then his right,
then up into his chest and down into his belly.

Ralph shrieked, "Doc, why all the incisions?"

"That's just the way the ball bounces."

Q: *What did the golfing caterpillar become when he grew up?*

A: *A putter-fly*

Q: *What do a musical conductor and a baseball statistician have in common?*

A: *They both know the score.*

A couple in Corpus Christi, Texas, named their son "ESPN" after the sports channel. The parents said the boy is okay with his name, but he's very jealous of his baby brother, "ESPN2."

-CONAN O'BRIEN

He spends so much time in the sand trap you'd
think he was in the cast of "Baywatch."

-TIM CONWAY

You observe a lot by just watching.

-Yogi Berra

Little Johnny dreamed of going to the zoo and pestered his parents about it day in and day out.

Finally his mother nagged his reluctant father into taking Johnny to the zoo for the day.

"So how was it?" his mother asked when they got home.

"Terrific," the father replied. "We had a great time. I was surprised at how much I enjoyed it."

"Is that true, Johnny?" his mom asked. "Did Daddy really have as good a time you?"

"Yeah, Mom ... He sure did– especially when one of the animals came running home at thirty to one!"

Doctor Dudley, toting his golf bag, was heading out of his dentist's office when his receptionist said, "Doctor, I have Mr. Arnold on the line. He has a toothache."

Dudley answered, "Tell him to call back tomorrow. I've got eighteen cavities to fill today."

Q: *What do you get when you cross a fighter with a telephone?*

A: *A boxing ring*

I don't like to watch golf on television.
I can't stand whispering.

                                        -DAVID BRENNER

OFF THE WALL

Humorous Graffiti from Lavatories of the Land

ATHLETE'S FOOT
COMES FROM ATHLETE'S FEAT

OLD BOWLING BALLS
WIND UP IN THE GUTTER

YOU CAN'T PLAY TENNIS
WITHOUT RAISING A RACKET

BASKETBALL PLAYERS TELL TALL TALES

A TIMEKEEPER IS A CLOCK-EYED MAN

OLD QUARTERBACKS NEVER DIE...
THEY JUST PASS AWAY

TENNIS PLAYERS HAVE A LOT OF FAULTS

SIAMESE TWINS LOVE DOUBLEHEADERS

BOXERS LOOK OUT
FOR THE RIGHTS OF OTHERS

There were just six seconds left on the clock of a tied pigskin contest. The quarterback threw a Hail Mary pass to the first-year wide receiver. He made a spectacular catch only to be hammered by the opposing cornerback. The ball fell loose and was picked up by a defender who ran the ball all the way for a game-ending touchdown. When the coach was asked about the heartbreaking defeat, he responded, "That's the way the rookie fumbles."

Mario Andretti has retired from race-car driving. That's a good thing. He's getting old. He ran his entire last race with his left blinker on.

-JON STEWART

A guy desperately wants to go to the Super Bowl so he goes to a scalper but can get only one ticket. He pays top dollar for a seat in the nose-bleed section, the second to last row of the upper deck. As the game begins, the guy's watching through his binoculars. He notices that there's an empty seat in the very first row, right on the fifty yard line. As the second quarter is about to end, he looks down and sees that the fifty yard line seat is still empty. At halftime, he makes his way down to the empty seat and asks the guy who's sitting in the next seat, "Is this taken?"

The guy replies, "No."

"Would you mind if I sit here?"

The other guy says, "Not at all. Go right ahead."

"I wonder why someone with a front row, fifty yard line seat wouldn't show up at the Super Bowl," says the first guy.

The second guy says, "Actually, my wife and I have come to every Super Bowl since 1967, but she passed away."

"Oh, gee, I'm sorry to hear that," says the first guy. "But couldn't you get a friend or relative to come to the game?"

"They're all at the funeral."

Q: Where did they put the matador who joined the baseball club?

A: In the bullpen

I feel like I'm the best, but you're not going to get me to say that.

-JERRY RICE

A college basketball coach scouted a high school player with unbelievable talent. The kid was 7'1" and had great offensive and defensive skills. Unfortunately, his academic skills didn't match. The coach begged the academic dean to admit the kid to the school. Finally, the dean agreed to let the kid in if he could answer three math questions.

The kid was brought in to the dean's office where he was asked the first question.

"What's two and two?" asked the dean.

The kid pondered for a few painful moments and finally replied, "Four."

"How much is four and four?"

The kid thought even longer this time before saying, "Eight."

"And now, for your final question, how much is eight and eight?"

The kid paused and paused and paused and then blurted out, "Sixteen."

With that, the coach begged to the dean, "Please! Please! Give him one more chance!"

A frustrated golfer, whose ball was lost in the rough, annoyedly asked his caddie, "Why must you constantly be looking at that pocket watch?"

The caddie responded, "Oh, it's not a pocket watch, sir. It's a compass."

It was Sunday morning and the clergyman should have been at church instead of the bowling alley. He rolled a 300 for his third game, looked up at the heavens and cried, "A perfect game and I can't tell anyone!"

I put Sugar Ray Robinson on the canvas - when he tripped over my body.

-ROCKY GRAZIANO

Three colleges are wooing a high school football star. The player shows up at Notre Dame where he notices a red telephone on the athletic director's desk. He asks, "What's that phone for?"

"Oh, that," replies the athletic director. "That's the hot line to Heaven."

"Gee, could I borrow it?" asks the football star.

"Sure, but it'll cost you 100 dollars a minute."

"Oh, that's too steep for me."

The player visits the University of Michigan next and sees a blue phone on the athletic director's desk.

"What's that blue telephone for?" the player asks the athletic director.

"That's our hot line to Heaven."

The football star asks, "Can I make a call?"

"Yeah, but you'll have to reimburse us 100 dollars a minute."

"Oh, gee. I don't have that kind of money. Thanks anyway."

For the third leg of his college visits, the football player goes to Notre Dame. There, he sees a gold telephone on the athletic director's desk. "What's that phone for?" he asks.

"That's our hot line to Heaven," says the athletic director.

"Mind if I borrow it?"

"Not at all, but we have to keep our costs down so I'm afraid I'll have to ask you to pay for it."

"And how much is that, sir?"

"Five cents a minute."

"Five cents a minute to call Heaven! Wow! How come it's so cheap?" asks the footballer.

The Fighting Irish athletic director responds, "Because it's only a local call."

Then there was the pro football bruiser who was offered seven figures to pen his autobiography. A year later, he turned in the story of his jeep.

A cat is watching a tennis match. Another cat strolls by and says, "Why are you watching that. Cats don't like tennis."

"I know but my father's in the racket."

There's a deep fly ball... Winfield goes back, back... his head hits the wall... it's rolling toward second base.

-PLAY BY PLAY ANNOUNCER JERRY COLEMAN

I can't really remember the names of the clubs that we went to.

-Shaquille O'Neal, when asked if he'd visited the Parthenon during his visit to Greece

That silver medal at the Olympics, that's something, isn't it? You get gold, you've won. You get bronze, "Well, at least I got something." But silver is basically saying, "Of everyone that lost, you were the best. No one lost ahead of you; you are the very best loser."

-Jerry Seinfeld

Q: Why do the Devil Rays play in a dome?
A: Because even God can't stand to watch.

There's no secret to winning the
Indianapolis 500. You just press the
accelerator to the floor and steer left.

-BILL VUKOVICH

Q: How does Brett Favre change a light bulb?
A: He passes the job to a receiver.